WAR, OVER EASY

Cover artwork by Mike Muench © 2018
located at mikemuench.com
First printing, 2018
ISBN 978-0692131336

for my whole family,
both by blood and by heart.

PREFACE

It was an early Monday morning in Brooklyn, New York during the pinnacle of winter's bullshit. Pete, my neighbor, was playing guitar loudly. It carried through the hollow roach-worn walls that separated us, and his drunkenness carried over from the night before. Friends of his were drinking on our co-joined balcony and marveling at the specks of ice that appeared to be shooting from the sun hanging low in the cloudless sky. I poked my head out to say my hello's and goodbye's. Pete called me into the living room to help him write a song. "J, give me your thoughts on this. It sounds a bit too Stone Roses, but if it worked for them it could work for me" he said in his slumping English accent. We had a beer, and pondered the efficacy of the song. Eventually 7 a.m. turned to 8 a.m., so I left.

The Avenue of Puerto Rico was lined with trash and the people shuffled along with their coffees from the broken bodega. Up ahead, the train tracks sat in plain view, zig zagging around the psychiatric hospital. As with every morning, I knew at any moment I would see my train pull up and pull off, dashing my hopes of catching it on time. This was a frightening thought, so I sprinted up all 68 glassy stairs and gracefully slipped on three of them. My ankle rolled, and my hands froze shut. I hobbled to the top of the outdoor train platform, missing the M line by one loud, "hey god dammit hold the door!" I was doomed to withstand another hour of the cold.

Within that span of wait time, wondering why this universe had to be cruel to a man who already had a cruel enough job, I received an email from my great aunt with a haiku that she had written. Attached to the email chain were my grandmother, mom, aunt, and a few others, all sending in their haikus. I didn't think much of it, as I wasn't a poet, but I wrote one back to the group anyway.

It was a contextual response to my great aunt's haiku, and it read:

My jonquil knowledge?
26 years in the dark.
Flowers, idiot.

This is the first I can remember ever giving a semblance of thought to a poem, let alone writing one. From that ugly haiku grew a passion, and I began exploring it every morning; slipping up those stairs, and prying my fingers apart to type all 17 syllables. This is how my journey began.

Some time in between that haiku and the finalizing of *War, Over Easy*, I went crazy.

I let my mind off the leash. I began walking through the city looking for stories. I entered little bars in the village, and got kicked out of a tiki pit stop, junkie haven. I got scratched by a stray cat and begged for money on the street. I got political. I became a recluse. I got very little sleep. I dated a couple of women who were lonelier than me. Those relationships went nowhere, and I went on to form the content of this book. I wrote some of these poems in between the haunting throes of utter boredom, and some on the playground bench outside of P.S. 140 Nathan Straus. Some of the poems I wrote at my job while the bosses were busy congratulating themselves. Some were written out on the East Lawn of Central Park after choking on hotdogs and washing them back with sunlight, and some were done while sick in bed, or while sick in love. All of them, though, are written for me, and to you.

In *War, Over Easy*, I do not relinquish my most honest mental corners to sell a product. These poems deal with the longest hills of personal sadness, and the highest points of bliss. They deal with the loss of friends and family, the loss and discovery of ourselves, and everything in between. Each piece is what it is, and I have no intention of revising any of them. If one of them isn't effective, then it will simply slip through the street drain with the rest of the hamburger wrapper poems. Maybe you'll love it and wear it on your body as a shawl or a tattoo, or you'll hang it on your wall, crooked, and your friends will tilt their heads to read it and go "hmmm" and that will be the extent of the poem's worth.

I want those who take this journey with me to understand me, and I want to know that I might understand them. All that I can promise is that my soul is buried within these sheets of paper. I assume that you are all here in search of your own, so maybe this will help guide you.

Cheers,
JH Hard
New York City, NY
May 12, 2018

Table of Contents

O N E

T W O

THREE

1

the sea speaks more honestly
to those willing to drown

burn me down

the heart is
what matters.

my body
the rest of me
is unimportant.

like the urn
the casket

it is a house
nothing more.

here is the address
go on
burn me down

but first reach inside
and save what matters.

revolution

let us rot quietly under the
rags of the morning.
take us out to the crumbling pew
past the dew that spills from
the ducts of
this grieving grass.

look at the world
as it really is. as it really
is.
do you see beauty
or do you see the truth?
green is a gray to the colorblind.

where we once were all in
we are now all out.

like the love,
so went the luck, the fortunes,
the friends, the baby, and the bathwater.

now all that remains
are these intertwined pinkies
and
this ammo.

daisies and fire

we know nothing
of who we
really are
until we skip through
daisies and
fire
and decide
in which to lie
down.

tulips

laid off
in the cold of spring
the winter never ends
global warming
(ha)
two pathetic weeks
of pay
and a W-2
coming in too late.
a fool who writes foolish
poetry full of hope
with a belly full of sickness
a disintegrating
twenty-something
with the mind of an octogenarian.
who would hire
such a prisoner?
an email from the old boss
saying "sorry, man."
I'm not your man, man.
I don't understand
the weekend anymore.
I'm sending out emails with
typos in abundance.
Tennessee never looked
so good.
it could be a fine idea
to head on back

and settle down with a
brown haired girl who laughs.
a blonde if I'm feeling
nostalgic.
now could be the chance
but I don't.
I just grind and grind
and write and grind.
the masochist in me tells
the nihilist to step aside.
usually when I tell myself
that nothing matters
that is when it all does.
if I am not everything
then I am nothing.
I grind and grind
and I only look up from
the pages to see
the bees among the
slouching tulips.
if they do not work
they die.
if they do not work
they die.

look at you now

do not bury
your skin
six inches under
cosmetic dirt.

your skin does not
need a coffin.
it is alive and
well.

every
pimple
freckle
blemish
scar

they dance
and scream out
for who you are.

and I look at you now

and I will always love
this you.

magenta cake and the
machine gun

this world is not for us
don't you see?

follow along with the razors
as they flay the night

as they cut into the wrist
of dusk's horizon

as the ribbons of moonlight
confetti down
shredding down
letting you down

don't you see?
this world is not for us.

how could it be
when
the beautiful die young
while the slime sleep through
the death of the day
and only awake
to force the
night to its knees without consequence?

this world is not for us.
don't you see?

we can only spend
what is left
of our stuttering days
as we know how.

taking in magenta cake
and the machine gun sorrow
and tilting softly into our wars
and

flushing the screenplays with the shit
and bolting up yesterday's news
and feeding the premature epitaphs
to the dogs
and

forging our love into lethal weapons
because it will be necessary
if we want to
survive
in this world that has never been
for us.

at a party in tribeca on a tuesday evening

little puffs
of cigarette smoke
above
all the pretty
people's
heads
like empty
thought bubbles
from which
the words had
spilled

and it is sort of a beautiful
thing to see but
still

empty.

the ball

puppies
and drunks with
leftover stamina from
the night   howl
as the sun
curls into view
revealing itself like a
curious beetle. the
horizon
squeezes
that bulging orange
into a glass   half-shattered.

and
for at least today
the earth is not flat.

nor are her eyes
in this bedroom.
I wax poetic, a couple of glossed
blue planets
darting
after each ray
of light

that wriggles
through cigarette holes

in a
Japanese blanket
that we have
stapled   up
pretending to be curtains.

yeah, soak it all in, Hard
every ounce of this moment
with her

because eventually
that sun will drop

and knowing you
so will the ball.

i d k

what is a poem
if it is not hated by
the happy?

what is a poem if
it is not dead on arrival
thrown into the fire
and mourned
by its creator?

what is a poem
if it is rewritten repeatedly
to appease the
selfish little consumer
who needs the writer to fix them
now now now?

what is a poem
what the hell is a poem

my fingers are striking these keys.
if I do it even harder
does that make it a poem?

can a poem quench the
magnetic, gripping, ripping
urges of a murderer?

should we march one down
to Rikers Island
and find out?

do the freaks and the romantics
all live and die by the
same credo in any given poem?

what do the psychos see
that the dull do not?

the words are just words
and if a poem is simply
a clump of words

who determines which
clump is to become immortal?

all of these questions are
important for my work

but here I go again

killing my dream of finding
beauty through writing.
killing all sanity
in the melting galaxy
of this kitchen corner.

killing these words because
they are not the immortal ones.

what you do when you feel blue

the days aren't always filled
with the proper words.

often they're spent feeling
sick

waking up to rain
breaking through the
cracks in the window
unraveling sheets
and a sadness that makes
my stomach
drop
to even think of it.

I turn on the tv to drown
the thoughts

I don't listen to enough music
because all of the words
find a way to relate
and crush me.

and especially now
it is silent as I write this
and my family is hundreds
of miles away.

and the girl has not yet
found her way to me
nor I to her.

but I'll be alright
and I'll jog along the
reservoir, blending into
a sun-drenched noon.

exercise is key.

the purpose for the struggle

I have kissed the darkest edge.
I have swallowed the burning sea.
I have clothed my eyes in dead flowers.
I have undressed my wilting bones.
I have held the screams of these veins.
I have sewed up what is left of this soul.

I have given all of this for a reason.
I have not known why.

but as the shadows close in
and these tourniquet nights tighten
I have begun to realize that I am more
prepared than they for this eternal fight.

self love

you stare into the mirror
disgusted
at the rolling field
of blackheads
that have
sprouted from
the dirt of living

as if
it were not
a blessing to be
alive
to bear such a field.

hell has coffee tables, too

I pinch myself to gauge
how close I am.
I shuffle toward
the cliff
to feel that I am still alive.
and
down below
the boneyard opens
its fragile
arms.
they know I am weak.

it is forever night in my heart
and the owls
know this, too.
they shut their eyes
and spin their heads from me
toward vomiting skies.

they can't look but
I have to.

and I pray that the devil
has not seen me
pacing
through his waiting room

but hell has coffee tables, too
so he has seen my
writings.
he knows the disease in this ink.
he has prodded through
the broken mind
of a man
a test subject
a research paper for his
burning shelves

and I am
sure he knows just the thing
to bring me home
to him.

pretend

we are dancing
and
singing and the
plane is going
down.

life is not easy
but we
can pretend

like we
did as
kids

lying in
the grass and

lying about
what we saw
in the clouds.

digging for the rats

I don't envy
better writers.

that they are better
means they are
even more
fucked in the head than
I.

I used to walk down
to a barge in Brooklyn
and climb below
the deck to kick through
the rocks and
the bums
and the trash
praying for
a stampede of rats to
swamp my body
just so
I would have something
to write about.
not that I want to be normal, but
that
surely isn't.
it's a well mind
that I envy

but those are usually wasted
on the dull.

those who skip through it all
without so much as an after thought
of after life or failure,
taking in the details of a single flower
in a field of millions and
marveling at it for existing.

I'm sure they want something
more than that empty bliss, but
the world
demands its role players.

so I guess I'll keep
digging for the rats

and the better writers
will keep being
even more fucked than that

and the well minds will
smile and
storm the rose fields

and maybe on an off day
we will all
step a bit out of line.

loneliness lives among
the masses

a gangly woman
jogging the river.
the neighborhood wacko
conquering the Gray bar
at a pale dawn.
a homeless kid
flipping through
Tolstoy on 14th.
a group at
the crosswalk huddled
together like strangers on an
elevator. an elevator
full of strangers
standing together
like 3rd grade children on
a field trip.
a CEO, a priest, and a criminal
walk into a bar
filled with deadpan
faces that walk out of it.
snails in gutters and
pigeons on bus benches
with transient figures that blur
away as the bus appears
and goes.

we all have
something in common
which is nothing.
individuals with thoughts
that have no true counterpart
criss crossing through rainy streets
with cracks in
sidewalks, usually
shoulder to shoulder
but always
alone.

the fluidity of us

it was easy when we broke
like waves.
calculated, often unable to
catch each other
but all the while
knowing
we'd get another chance and
everything would be right.

with that safety net
she and I reveled in our
sanctimonious
brawls.

egg salad sandwiches and crackers,
volcanic screaming and
ginger ale.

then
making love out by the fire pits
and garbage bins
on the beach.

I always thought
it could just be a big lie,
this cycle of love and torture
between us.

it couldn't be realistic.
eventually it would all come to
a head, maybe
in the form of
joint aneurysms or
symphonic murder.

it was only a theory
until a cool day in early October
when
the waves didn't break.

the horizon lay still
like a field of corpses after battle
and I cried for the first time in a year
at the finality before me.

you were gone. I knew that.
so did
the sky turning black.
so did the seagulls
turning their backs
to the ocean.

and I knew, the only thing left to do
was to return my heart to the sea
to heal in the salt
to rest in the
silence.

fix the world

it came to me
like a shot to the spine
that we are all
allied with the bomb
in this war on love.
is this our fate?
to be the exorcists of
compassion?

self-loathing
but self-centered
as we watch society melt
like a snowflake
in the ocean.

tell me how many rotations
of this earth
we should waste until we save it?

gravediggers
stack your shovels with sand and spill
it into every hour glass
because the seconds
have grown
shorter
and there is
no time to think.

are you up for it or
are you snoring
through the noon sun?

the larks in the ghettos haven't given up
garbage men in spurring winters haven't given up
carnations in abandoned landfills haven't given up

I haven't given up. you?

cry

there can never be
too much
rain

for it is always a good
thing
to let it all out

even for the gods.

there is more to it all

the cat is ending its shift at the window sill
and the sun is heading home for the evening.

the voices of the street are growing a little drunker,
from weaving like silk through the neighborhood alleys,
to bouncing and crashing off of their walls.

my pupils dilate with the moon.
the man on it yawns, and the ocean tide
is off somewhere moshing with its friends.

and I am eight lines into this, now nine
and I have not yet figured out how to relate it to you
which was my original intent.

I have described the ascent of another night. and it
subtly depicts a lack of you, sure, but I am beginning to

understand that our lives are not always wasted
without that one person, but it can be wasted
in many other ways. for example

by writing all the way to line seventeen of a poem
meant for a woman who broke your heart, while

you miss out on the beautiful night
that you had originally begun describing.

for erin, at her grave

open up, great sky.

I want to see you for
what you really are.
go on and gust your
boisterous gales.
I want to smell
the toxins
and the bullshit.

I want you to show your
true colors.
not this facade
of baby blue innocence.

show me your blood reds
dripped from fangs
and deep purples
like spurting veins
and clotted clouds
swirling through a porcelain
toilet

show me the poison
the venom
show me the agenda
and the lives that you

claim as your own.

you are not beautiful.
you take.

liquor me up, great sky.
because I want to
forget that

she
lives somewhere
within
you now.

and as loud as I scream to you
you won't let her
come back to me
but

I have heard that
eventually
the sky must fall
and when that time arrives
it will be me
who brings you down.

alive

right now
we are all alive.

sick
writing
kissing
screwing
killing
laughing
running
crawling
sleeping
vomiting
eating
breaking
punching
mending
loving

if your heart is
currently dissolving into
nothing
you are still alive

if you are climbing
a tall crane
from which to jump

or to hang
you are still alive

if you are breathing in
another person
frightened
as you realize

that your breath
is her breath
and there is no going back
you are still alive

if you are clinging
to the rose
as all of the birds
retreat south
you are still alive

do not ever
let yourself go
until you have accepted
that you are still alive.

good one

red light New York
west of 5th
on the
verge of dawn.

buildings lean on
one another to rest, and

cabs pulse by
painted yellow heat waves and
in them are
the lucky ones

and all of the leftovers are
stuck
flapping
their arms toward
the stars

and they are hanging out on
the side of the world
waiting their turn

and the prostitutes are looking for
a way out

and the lovers are giving up

and the deranged
are playing with
the atoms in the mist

and all of the above
are fulfilling the cliché of a
place

we
are told
never sleeps.

and I,
up at 4am,
am writing about
the most written about
city in the world

being the biggest cliché
of them all.

proverbs from the coffin
(for jeff)

10 years ago, drunk, watching calico clouds
swim by on the back nine
at Saunders Ferry Park in our hometown, my
buddy asked me
what's your perspective on death, and
I had no answer for him.
we were just kids, you know?
well, he has since passed away, so
I want to answer him now:

I.
when it is time
with great reluctance
we will be sucked into the earth
like the rain, and
the worms will belch back the bones.
this calms me
because there is nothing more calming
than the truth, and there is nothing
more truthful than this.
and while my sentiment here may not be for
everyone
the death part is.

II.
etched into the cherry finish
six feet beneath the living, the spirits
write what was left unsaid.
the regrets, the love notes, the lyrics.
it is seen only by the silence
and sometimes the grave robbers
but they keep those secrets.
the integrity of the dead is not to be trifled with.

III.
the living become ashamed of their living
and often look for a taste of the alternative.
but I have been buried in the white web
of the alternative along with the kicking flies
and I beg them to reconsider.

IV.
if you are loved
you will find yourself in a
beautifully crafted mahogany box
with complimentary cushions
of velvet to keep your skull
comfortable for the long sleep.

and if you are unlovable
the strangers blazing down I-65
late to a PTA meeting
will notice you

waterlogged in a ditch
and they won't stop.

V.
the ugliness of denial is that it
is beautiful;
that's it.

and one day, all of this will sneak up on you
but for now
you don't have to worry about it.

because this is just my take on
the winter of life
my personal proverbs from the coffin
and it is summer
and your hammock
is waiting.

rising

this earth
will drag you back down
to it
but just promise me
that you will continue to rise.
the sun and the moon
cannot be in this
alone.

some things we just accept

to be a deer in
a forest so deep
no man could find me

seeing the sun
through the trees
enjoying such simplicity as
the warm rays, like fingers
sifting through my fur

or to be a rock flying down
highways in space, free
unbothered by dirty soles
of cheap sneakers
in a scorched
parking lot.

to be these things
is a thought probably
shared by fools, both sane
and lucid

but all this man
can really be is a quiet
set of meat and bones
stewing in a chair
writing vaguely a poem.

bittersweet monkeys

hawks of sabotage sink low
tonight.

the ever-rare
successful day is
behind us.

I lie in
sarcoline drapes
turtled out neck. twisted
eyes
watching

as
the lilies bloom
between the cracked skin
and corners of
her
smile

each lip
pushing out sharpened words
through parting tones
about silver suns
toppling over and rupturing
entire days

but we share
more
timidly
about parents
that never cared.

and we drink down
the roaring
flood

of each sentence
working to cauterize
the past

until
we find ourselves dangling
from
the tip of the moon

like a pair of
bittersweet monkeys
in love
safe
and slowly becoming
unbothered

by the
world
below.

rambling about meaning

send your heart
into the fray
and let it
come out stronger.

take trips
you can't afford
to an exotic country
and bury your soul
into its soil
so it will always remember
you.

kiss your mother.
hug your father.

answer the phone when
your grandparents call
because they're still
here
if only for another blink.

and if nothing else,
you should be learning all you can
from them.

wisdom doesn't follow us to the grave.

read old literature.
watch a movie in French.
french a girl at the movies.
let her boyfriend
punch you in the face.

it's good
to know what it's like to
take a hit
every now and then.

it reminds us
that we aren't invincible.

remember that your brother
or sister
is your best friend.

not your vomit partner
at 3 a.m. in a shady pub.

speaking of pubs
I got kicked out of one
after a friend's wedding
because I slapped the
bartender
across the face
(for good reason)

they threw us all into the street
and I had never felt so free.

slap the deserving.
exit toxic environments.
and then
wake up the next day
and look for more meaning.

search hourly for it.

you may not find it right away
and that's ok
because

you can write about
what meant something
in your past, that led you here
as I am doing right now.

and maybe people will read it
and appreciate it

even if it doesn't really
mean anything
to them.

2

stuck in between the teeth of time

little trampoline

too many warm evenings with you
to forget.
I bought this little trampoline for us
and
you laid your head on it
mostly. sublime, awkward, ears toward
ground and sky.
your cigarette ash would blend
into the morning
mist, yes
I remember well.
you inherited your mother's
smile
and I thanked her silently
every time that you
did.
and your father's strength
unstoppable
like rivers from your
mind, heart, fingertips. he
left us all
just 14, yes
I remember well.
too many warm evenings with you
to forget.

cyclical sea

I will live like the ocean.
I will never settle.
I will stay quiet
then rage with the
sky. on the lonelier days
I will roll onto the
shore
and look for you.
when I do not find you
I will roll back out.
and then
as I have done for so long
I will repeat.

harmony

our twin smiles settle
under
a charcoal moon

these
siamese hearts purge
the demons that
we could
never
shake alone and

God caters this
moment
with cocktails of patient
rain

and we clank our glass
and discuss
the struggle
it took to arrive here
at this harmony

taking everything in
but nothing for granted.

christopher street coming down

yelling at the sky
in the center
of Christopher Street
because we are free.

the fountain of youth
has tipped and it is
showering
over us

and the nightshift security says

"get out of the street you crazy assholes"

and people are running
for cover from the
deluge
under bodega awnings
and umbrellas and coats and
I feel sorry
because

I do not think
that they got the memo and
now they are missing out
on all these years.

the garbage man's guilt

I heard the garbage men
early in the morning
before
the sun
interrupted the city.

one was howling about
cheating on his wife.

"I screwed that girl from the bar
the other night. Jenna was her name, I think.
can't take it back.
wouldn't want to. she was tight.
the wife didn't even know
I was gone."
he bragged.

they laughed.

he was loud
handling the cans.
louder than usual, I suppose.

sort of thrashing about, really
like a drowning man.
maybe he was. or

maybe he was agitated
because
he hadn't slept in days.

guilt does that to a man.

garbage or not.

demons

your demons never knock.

they just appear on
the doorstep of your
brain.

with a grin and a
bottle of fine wine
they step
through the threshold
of your being.

"where's your couch?"
they demand
as they stretch out
across your thoughts
and make
themselves at home

again
with that grin
and a glass of sweet wine.

and then
without warning
they set fire to your curtains
kick the dog

punch your neighbors
and quit your job.

"it's important to turn away your demons."

Stephan Jenkins said that
I think.

summer shorts

I lost it, oh
I've lost it all

I try to bleed
with desperation
my feelings onto paper

but the dogging nights
have vanished
into august
rivers

the lovers haven't left
so much as
they've
just stopped showing
up

the hair has left me
the knees are
threatening
next

the almighty mirror
has no reason to lie
anymore.
it has served its

false purpose
and it can go now
too.

my point is that
really
all you can do is appreciate
what little is left. like

the popping laugh
in a newborn
or a windy gust reaching up
your summer
shorts.

this cerebral war

you can't find happiness without first
living through the darkness.

they are inextricably linked.

they are brothers and sisters
of this infinite cerebral war.
they need each other to survive.

so when that darkness presents itself
in all of its sadness and anger and defeat
do not run
do not hide
do not ignore it.

confront it with spectacular fire.

because once you come out on the other side of it
(and you will)

it will only make the light that much warmer.
the happiness and the love
that much sweeter.

to the old days

before the time of
turf war
and
clutched rosary

asphalt dogs
staring into suns
and sons staring into
coffins.

before the velvet thick
of the artery
sprayed poetically
onto
the turntable
distorting all symphony
into chaos.

before the Indian Strawberry
tricked the infant.

before the
broken tail lights led
all of this
into the fog, we
existed in a bubble.

watching moons rise
on stoops
and cigarettes go down
in flames.

talking over each other

on fold-outs eating
cold toast
and bursting with pride.

we really were in love then
weren't we?

clara

I survived every day
by thinking of you
and then I died
doing just the same.

anonymous girl in the quarters

hot flickering piles
of human waste
lined the streets of the
French Quarter.

it is hilarious to me that
people come here
for fun or passion.
they probably leave instead
with hepatitis
inside of empty wallets.

Razzoo's bar was glowing and
I was purple
in its shadow

smoking things all alone
and wishing for rain
to feel clean again
and

through the dewy crowd of heads that
bobbed like stock prices
there was a girl
(there is always a girl, isn't there?)

she was waiting for something.

not me.

probably for God
or poutine
or rivers to melt.

but she approached anyway
and pulled me
into the straw alley
and I didn't have time
to look
at her face and

we danced slow but strong
to Sam Cook's voice
that was stumbling
through the
street from off in the distance.

and she told me
that she felt hate
inside of my heart
and I joked "what heart"
and she
said that she could see
the darkness
through my eyes
and I asked her what color they were
and she said brown
and that
was wrong

and I told her she
smelled like forgotten oceans
and
she said which one and I
told her that I couldn't remember

and there was sweat
on her back
and tears
near her lip
and I was shocked that I had found

porcelain in
this neon slush and with that

the drunken dawn ripped us apart
and I slept in the car to the airport
and dreamt that I was
forgetting something.

a name
a name

it is always the most important thing
that we fail to accomplish.

to myself

movies alone
I have seen them all.

I recite the lines
with the people
on the screen.
there would
not be many lines
for them to recite of
me.

I keep quiet
mostly.

writing the words
missing meals

losing sleep loving
the girl who loves another.

this is a movie that
no man should
have to see.

how i remember her

her laughter
shook her body
like a willow
tree in a storm

her chest rose and fell
and her hands
shot to the sky
and
crashed
repeatedly
into her knees

and
for a split second
I feared she
was having a seizure
until
she snapped out of it
and said

"can we laugh like this forever?"

and I did not see
why not.

crusted suns

I chase those
little moments of you
still.
my feet have bloodied
and I can't stop.

that imperfect kiss
under waning bulbs, lined
along sidewalks
slithering infinite
and our years
that lived from it.

it left behind wet shadows
ripe and deep and ours.

it is within these shadows
that I have existed since
you have gone.

and though the crusted suns threaten
and dig through the city
in search of me, I will not
give into them.

but time is a maybe. time is a leech
in the dead of the desert.

time takes
from things that take time.

and I know that these shadows will
eventually dry up

and I will be left without you
again.
exposed.

old man, we'll be fine

I saw a man
reading in the rain.

his book had been soaked

pages shriveling like
wet
lasagna noodles.

I asked him if
he would like
an umbrella.

he said
"if it's God's will that these words fade away
then so be it."

I thought this was profound
and I told him so.

he asked why;
I shrugged.

I walked on toward work and
dropped my umbrella in solidarity.

timber

the suffering
comes
in waves

and I am
a naïve child
splashing
in the calm
broken peripherals
humming loud
a broken song
for the vultures

as the wave towers
over me and
no one says
timber.

going down singing

we grew mad with love
deep in the fire of summer

soft beds afloat on ember
flowers afraid to graze our skin

the mourning doves burning up
in the sky
going down singing

and oh, my love, it is so hard
to conceive
of a winter

even though we both know that
these winds cannot hibernate

within the trees
forever.

a conversation on a highway

passenger seat
leather
cracked, cold

her lips, her heart
the same

in cars
always in cars

why

why do we do this.

maybe

maybe
the galaxy is just litter.
maybe
the moon and the
planets are just marbles
and cereal puffs that
God had
forgotten to clean up
after a party one
evening.
maybe
we are just
the mold growing on
a dust particle
and soon
a broom will come
sweep us back into
nothing.

the pier

it was a blast
and the day was long

ferris wheels and fair food

if we vomited we aimed the sick
at the downers
and if we were to die, we would wish
each other well

the amusement pier
was lit with endorphins

tourists fist fighting
used needles on the beach and
tiny kids cheering at the
magic of it all

beautiful people,
wandering gutter punks,
all with funnel cake woven between teeth
smiling at the collapsing sun
off of
the crooked coast line.

washed up

Steven is belly up
passed out on
the Florida shoreline.

the dizzy little crabs pull
at his toes.
the dogs see a new toilet.

the women
see
a future husband.
no, not Steven.
the guy stepping over him.

but now the April moon
is marching toward the
horizon
and I sink into sand
watching

and writing this
for my washed up friend
who, thankfully,
beat me to it.

the clarity in a moment of shock

the morning
has its first wave of calm
the sky is big
and lazy behind the sun

the birds
go on about
their freedom

the wind shuffles through the
weeds that grow
between the cracks
in the sidewalk
and

in the middle of the street:
a car wreck

the arbiter of
this visceral peace

blood
spattered along
the pearlescent white
of the door
the recreation
of

a Pollock
perhaps?
(no, it's too clean)

smoke
waves like
English royalty

toward a hypnotized
audience

car and body parts
stacked Jenga blocks

a work of art
a lapse
in routine
the beauty of madness
before the panic
sets in.

eventually we all get there

we chased the silence
in
wood-paneled basements.
all of the lights
in them
were

green and
we looked
like the slime
we always knew we were.

threatened by a clear September
night full of stars
that we didn't deserve

their brilliance was meant
for those that had done
deeds
and we were
just children of the
smog.

and love called in at 2 a.m.
Jessica's voice
asking for the junk.

I'd never met a woman more
desperate to die
in the arms of a man
or
in the veins of her arms.
which one
depended on the time
and none of us were safe from that

but safe is a cage
and animals
shit in those
so instead we melted before the night
and let the darkness
swallow.

we were lucky cats;
the scourge of Death and God.

we had beaten the odds and
ourselves

and if you were to ask if
I'd do it all again

I'd run for the hills.

older

the older I get, the more I realize that
this life is not about me.
it is about bleeding for your loved ones
because they would do the same.
it is about bidding farewell to every sunset.
it is about breathing in the river as it flows
and respecting what lives within it.
it is not about us, but about loving all of the
beautiful things surrounding us.
because all of those things are
what give us this life
anyway.

can of worms

a hundred years could go
and I still would not be able
to picture
myself here, writing and pitching
this screenplay about
my hometown.

about the friends I have lost.
watching one
take his last breath
pool side
at the Comfort Inn
off the highway shoulder
that has since been bulldozed.

watching the rest of them
trail off
to the furthest corners of
sanity and America
and never looking back to even
smile or scream.

and when I watched the studio
reject that screenplay
like a horsefly
inching toward a plate of cookies
never could I have pictured

my eyes
filled with tears
of pure
fucking
relief.

eighteen luck

from Hendersonville, Tennessee
I moved on across
the earth.

when I left
your sister rolled her eyes and told me to
come back next decade
so here I am.

I noticed your old car still had
the dent from
when we fell into it
lit on malibu
clanking our smiles.

it rushed back to me then.
rain on the eyelashes
kisses in the thousands
road maps traced on skin
road maps fading.

your hair was blonde.
snowy white in the sunshine
through the sunroof as we smoked
chamomile in Devon's cherokee.
we were immortal
to the days.

and Friday nights
would reverberate through
the church parking lot that
kept all of our secrets safe.
and when we summoned
the fortune teller on main street

she predicted that
by the twilight of our youth
we would have more than this.
that liar.

but hopefully you've noticed by now
yes, this is for you.
the road maps that you and I
traced and studied
those years ago, led me to

New York, Atlanta, Milan
and your window
looked out over south orchard street
and never took its eyes away.

but I will be back there again in July.
and I'll stand off that street
and from your window
sad eyes will wave
goodbye

because I've lost a lot of women
in a handful of towns

in approximately
a dozen
different ways.

but I've not had as much success
getting them back.

jack's ear

barbershop in the glow of a Sunday's noon
Jack's regular guy Manny raps off
about Lolita,
his mistress, aged forty.
Terrence is sweeping up hair next to them.
browns, reds, blondes, greens and blues
all swirled together and

he asks Manny how to spell that name
Looo-liii-taaa
like he had never heard it before.

"I'm 63 muthafucka. I forgot how to spell
somewhere between Disco and Dr. Dre."

he continues scissoring and sculpting
through Jack's temples with the
instincts of an artist, still reeling though
from the night before, drunk
with his new woman in the bowling alley
bumping cocaine and dancing.

Jack smells it all over him when
that stench of wild youth cut through
the sprays and gels
and
talcum powder machine guns.

"I felt young again, Jack! as young as you."
he says, flipping his feet
as if he were tap dancing over hot coals.

"she's a gem, I swear. she even let me watch the
Yankees game while we were going at it.

can you believe th-"

suddenly, a slip of that artistic instinct,
and in the middle of his monologue,
Manny cuts Jack's ear.

25 dollars every week over the past year.
cash from his pocket, directly into Manny's
and now
he has begun taking body parts.

the talcum was phosphorus red
clumped up on
the edges of his face, and the
reggaeton
drowns out the fury.

the workers splash alcohol on it
and some gets in Jack's eye.
he can barely see the door as he scrambles for it
saying

"thanks guys, see you next week!"

old habits.

he hops a cab to the hospital
and gets stitched up.

so, if you're reading this, Manny:
Jack wants his money back.

you can keep the ear.

saviors and saltwood

and here, I
cruise down Saltwood
radio at full lung
fire feathered on my
breath in
the
satin evening.

the purple lake in the sky
sparkled in sync
with the notes and kicks
of Thelonius spreading
through the car.

stars dancing the samba
foxtrot
drunk
entertaining the only way
they know

the show is free, they never get paid,
then they
explode and die
but I never liked to imagine them as
balls of violent gas.

and now, I park in an empty field behind

an indolent church

God used to live here
still does
probably on his days off

and through the wind
a croak of desperation
the church speaks
of its desire to save us
and the stars stop dancing
and say
"us too"
and the music wants to
save itself

but if everything is ok
then there would be nothing
left to fix
so I simply ignore it all.

life is more exciting
this way.

better days

stored behind
tired, weathered skin
and brittle ribs

strangled within
chicken wire veins

you will find
this heart.

it has seen
better days

but I swear by the
words standing bold
on this page

that it will see them
again.

awake

I am tired.
I am so tired.

I have watched
shackles of wealth
drip from faucets

and caves form in honor
of tyrants

and countries burn in pursuit
of the insurance

and friends long since buried
among
the shit and the worms
forgotten
like
a plastic bag
tumbling
low in the canyons.

and the seas
are a cruel joke.
all show, no function
as our insides dry up
and we become its sand.

and our hair falls south
for the winter
and our eyes look north
for an answer, yet

we are left with
no time to ask the question.

yes
I am so very tired.
but I am
awake.

not today

it is a bleak day when
I can't write.
even bleaker when
I can.

distance be damned

we are continents apart, and still
I can breathe you in.

how can love be so present always?

it does not fall from the sky
like an exhausted bird.
it does not fade
like the scent of the lilac field
upon nearing the city limit sign.

how does it not fade!
it just goes forward
powers forward.

a little red sailboat in the eye
of a hurricane
the camel skipping through
the gut of the desert
the knife into the back of the enemy
the feet into the mud
of the earth, God
into it all.

it is truly madness, this love
this persistence of you
always here

always there
on the tips of my senses, the cliffs
of my mind.

but if there was no madness in love
then there would be no sanity
in anything.

mr. happy

walking through the city
dressed like Dracula
eating over cooked
egg wraps in
a morning fog

last night, I wrote
a strongly worded love letter
to Death before
I slept
but obviously it rejected me
as I am awake
and writing this
nonsense.

the Reaper is a conspiracy.

he is just life,
bored
with nothing new
on the docket.

and oh well
because the cars keep
slugging by me anyway
with happy idiots
listening to

self-help tapes and
jazzing over blue jean
Fridays

and soon
they will crash and so will I.

probably in ditches
when
the fog is lifted.

the survival of richard

there was quiet enough
on that invisible beach
in The Gambia.

he reemerged at the sunrise bar

with a turtle shell heart
and a molasses mind.

by that time, the sun
was the only one
who knew
or cared
that he existed anymore.

he carried on daily
incoherently drunk

standing up, falling down
standing up, eating sand
vomiting at the water line.

he spent days recovering from
the love he let die, and he spent
nights recovering from the days

while the moon beat him down

and black-winged kites
shat on his skull
and the ocean
asked too many questions
about the girl.

as if he would ever
tell it anything. as if

answering
would ever
bring her to that place
that trap
that he had mistaken
for a sanctuary.

and then i said —

you and I are
spiders sliding down
the walls of a soda bottle
beneath a
tightening cap

you and I are the nights and days still
closing in all around
like
a hi-five, a tapioca sky
turning into a sherbet dawn
you and I are settling between
the machines of time as it rotates on
to squash our little love.

you and I are cherry-flavored rat poison.
you and I swallow down the blackbirds.

you and I are the silencers
on this loaded gun
and
of
our own loaded egos.

you and I are
you and I
and

don't act like you aren't enough for this
and I won't act like we aren't chained
together
for the long haul.

it's you and me, babe.

get used to it.

the end of an era

the rain began to fall and
I looked at my watch:

3 hours left for us.

the bodega was more humid
than usual
so I sat outside under the neon face of it
with the fruits.
the Mexicans fanned out in chairs
to my left and right
and spoke of politics
and hard up nights
in Puerto Vallarta
and
I understood little inflections
here and there but
I wished I had listened in
Señor Mear's Spanish class a
little more instead of flirting
with Lauren
in our native tongue.

then I witnessed the men laughing
which I understood even less.

and soon after, I left out

and paced down the sidewalk
where it held the puddles
like fountains
and in them I could see that the
street lights were out
and I glanced again:

2 hours until our end.

when she finally called
she was high.
her voice was buzzing
sort of how you'd imagine
a Hummingbird's to be.

and I could tell
she didn't know me anymore.
she knows the old me.
the older looking me.
the thief. the low life.

"we never got that coffee." I said
and she brushed it off as an
inconsequential act.

but things become clearer over coffee

and sometimes entire pasts are
forgiven, forgotten
in between the sugar and
the cream.

sometimes.

instead, we hiked to my place
and sat back in the gloom
pounding the TV with
stone glares.
chipping away at the moment.

and as the last hour disappeared
she said to me

"do you think it all turned out this way
for us in another dimension?"

I had nothing to say and we fell asleep
to the sound of the sirens
and the crazies...

when I awoke, time was up.
the ceiling was
still water-damaged.

she was
of course
gone. and I realized

there is no divine intervention
or radical change in
your critical moments with someone.
we are
who we are.

there is no check-point in our progress.
we live how we live
and things end
just as well.

the next few hours, days, years
without her
will putter by.

I'll eat fast food. watch the TV.
sleep too much. fight with the
landlord.

and then
when the rest of it comes

Mrs. Pratt will walk her dog
down Crosby street, across Howard
and the mailman will come
a little too late.

**i woke up this morning in a field
and wrote this**

aren't we so lucky
when
the snow stings
and the sun
chills
to know that
life can be
a bit
of
everything?

goodbye, cannibal sunset

this life will not last forever. neither will
                this night
neither will this song, neither
                will my knees
knocking together with yours.

                goodbye, cannibal sunset
hello, tremulous moon
                though
                                you will not last either.

but it fills me with hope that
                time is just as free
                                to come and go
as we.

                and all you and I can do is dance
                                while it is all here.

3

and so, the heart
scooted aorta first
across the splintered floor
toward its destiny

we'll be back

we were dysfunctional.
colloquial chaos.

screaming at dawn.
war, over easy.

afternoons, we rented hotels
for fun
almost weekly
and you would wonder
how many sad sacks had
killed themselves
on the beds.
the stains were invisible.
the pain probably, too.

I can't tell you how many times
I wanted
to
throw up
because of how much
I loved you.

the other women just made me happy.
there is nothing duller
than that.

screaming at dusk.
war, under amused moons.

don't you dare forget.
we'll be back.

bar napkin poem

here I sit
piss drunk at the
Blue and Gold bar in
the village.

Kamikaze Jane
across the way
is tearing into my soul
and she knows it.

she tells me to fuck off
with her smile
she lights a cigarette
with her laugh
she puts it out in my eye
with a wink

and I'm letting it all happen
inviting it through
drooling smiles.

poor schmuck.
drink up.

the avenue of puerto rico

a sweat bead quickly
rolls down her neck
past her chest and
I wonder why it
does not take
its time.

night on the town

drinks toss
and turn
in our stomachs

I look at you
and come undone

like the buttons on
your
dress in the
moonlight, in the dark

dancing furiously
shaking our
hair

trying to rid it of the
smoke
that came home
with us

only to find it stuck
within the fibers
of our clothes

and clothes are stupid
anyway.

blue-eyed morning

the morning comes like
dust to the shelf.

quiet, settling surrender
then all at once.

we peel back our heavy lids
to find that life has
reset

and across these rivers
of sheets
I see in you
that there cannot
ever again
be
a blue day

because your eyes have taken
sole possession of
that color.

taxi song

we wear each other down
in the hollows
of this aging city and
what we leave behind on that
sidewalk
will be gone tomorrow.

Sarah
pavement blazer
intrepid girl, I wonder
what her taxi song
is.

I know we all have
that one that we need to hear
while we tilt our heads
to rest on backseat
windows

and stare at the
blurry humans and little
circus lights that
continue
us
in separate directions
from each other.

flamenco sketches
pulls at my heart currently

and I mourn the beauty
of our night together
and know
that we are growing older

and that our moments
are fleeting even when we aren't.

and one day
another kid will be
in love in this cab and he will
have his taxi song whispering on
for another Sarah

and that too
will fleet.

cold roses

cold roses
lay behind her ear

thorns dug into
skin

patternless
streams of red

flow
down

to silk shoulders while

the garden rots
under
her toes
and

it is only Tuesday.

a fruitful day it was

we laughed with a snort and
drank plenty of water and
we took the park like
Columbus, but kind
and we triggered all
the street lamps when
the sun got bored
and we ate pierogies by the
Brooklyn shipyards
and held greasy hands
and we were none the wiser
to the ships floating in
or the stains on our shirts
or to the perils of
humanity on the
outskirts of
our day.

carrying on

let your heart
beat the odds.
and if you can't
find the
strength for that
right now
at least let your heart
beat.

dizzy

it was
a fine day
but I lived it
dizzy

the cars are too fast
so are the women

the thoughts of you spin
a little
too tightly

work crawls by
in a snailing lethargy

i don't eat enough food
(vended chips don't count)

the sun and the moon
tango too slowly
the dial on these years
ticks too often

decades
to days,
millenniums to months
looking for you again within

the swirling snow

looking for you again through
rolling spokes and
taxi hubcaps

I'll look for you again
within the city's maze when

my vision
adjusts

I'll wait for you
through the neon signs
touching the streets with their
inconsistent glow
and through turnstiles
and the train cars
that criss cross
aimless

I'll try to wait for you
to live dizzy
again.

first thing

to kiss you
in the morning when
the light has
exposed every pixel
of my flawed
face

with
the breath of death
lingering on
my lips
and trusting that
you accept it all.

there is nothing braver
in this moment.

fight

I fight
the good fight
and
survive the bad

and then

I go home and
love you
with
what is left.

excuses we frequent

my eyes roll
down the length of the bar
checking out all
the drunk, swollen faces
frowning
in a sad row like
a police lineup
where

everyone has done something
wrong.

I wonder often why we think
this is the solution

brooding in dimness and drenching
our insides alongside
no one
also known
to the more hollow patrons as
everyone.

why this place?
is it the fengshui?

the bathroom
is flooded and

the dart board has "dick"
scribbled on it.

someone sneezes and it is
the first
sound of the entire
night.
I almost cheer for this achievement.
but instead

I collect my things
and spin out the door, past
the red neon sign that
had drawn me in
and I tell myself "never again"

and across the street I see another
neon sign
but
it's ok

because this one
is blue.

loves me not

with our eyes closed
we let the sun
set over the old
windmill. one glass
of wine
two
then five
we drank ourselves
into romantic isolation.
scattered petals of
blue and pink led down
to where the sand
met the greenery. we
didn't remember
making such a mess
but I imagined
it was you
acting like a kid
"he loves me, he loves me not"
over and over until
you got it right.

return

I did not miss the part
where I should
miss you.

oh, I certainly did and
do.

I have gone straight to the wine.
the women in our bed.
the sensibilities, timid
in the morning
and weeping into
the twilight.

my brunette symphony
paint chip moles
disco eyes

how do we do this?

it is all brand new and broken.
I cannot return it

but you can.

memorial garden backyard

it is ironic
this stigma of rain.

we call it
depressing

while
right under
our nose
it gives a flower
the courage to
emerge
from its bud.

kelly

it's 2am and I'm going to tell you
about Kelly.

oh, Kelly

we smoked cigarettes and
drank rum in the back
of the club room
at Samba
as often as a sailor on the lam.

she was a handsome woman
looked sort of like
a man

I used to kiss her
anyway
because she had jokes
and heart
and it all came out
the deeper we
swam in the rum.

she used to pull me into
her like a dead body to the furnace
and say
"let me see more of you, J"

and I never knew
what that really
was supposed to mean
and we would go back to
laughing and kissing and swimming
in rum.

and nights would pass
like nausea at sea

the music fading away through
pinhole memories

and more and more we would resort to
the laughs and kisses
and rum.

until one day she put her cigarette
out on my shirt sleeve
and walked off and screwed
the Samba bartender in the
back of a cab.

she hated me because
there was
still something that I wasn't showing her
and maybe she had a point
anyway, because

this piece of writing
is all that I have to show.

resurfacing

battle stains
souvenir souls
drowning ghosts

she
resurfaces
and so do the memories.

they
hang from my ears
thawing out now
and the
blood of open wounds
dives
toward
the Terracotta rug.

the regret in this room
in my head
hides poorly
like a young child's heart
in a first puppy love
and I believe
once my thoughts are clear

it will be
revealed that none

of these memories
are really
what
I remembered them
to be, but
I will get drunk and
tell them
to someone who doesn't care
anyway.

I'll hand them
a few rotten words
from a rotten
fellow
with nice teeth

and I will probably be lying
through
them.

3 minutes, 51 seconds

I heard a song and it
made me think of you.

the song ended and that
made me think of you
too.

trapped and happy

our apartment
was more of a cave.

curtains like thick
dripping tongues
chugging light and
coughing up the darkness.
it pressed against us
a black ball pit.
Chucky Cheese without the
rainbows.
you and I left alone to
thrash at the bottom.

sensory deprivation
is real
and we lost our minds within it
for a little bit

which turned out ok, because
that was one less thing.
possessions are hell.

but we still smelled and tasted
like us. and I
still couldn't get you to stop
holding my feet with yours.

two birds, one tombstone

I recommend kissing
in a cemetery.

find the oldest
tombstone around
sit on it and
kiss her or
kiss him or
kiss them.

because the oldest
tombstone is
the least visited.

and all of us
even ghosts
need company.

and all of us
even kids
need privacy.

2:37am

I spoke to
Manhattan last
night.

it
answered with horns
and sounds
of
soft conversation
on fire
escapes.

it cried
a little and
laughed with thunder.

then it told me
that
you still love me
but
I didn't believe it.

though it hadn't lied
thus far.

when

the swells of the sea
form
into question marks
that answer themselves
upon the shore
where my feet have
sunken
deeper
into the sand.

I watch
the grains slip
between my toes
like

an hour glass
calculating the moments
until your
arrival

whenever
if ever
that may be.

just walking

violet lips
a violent jawline
sharpened further
by the shadows
of her neck and

shoulders broad like stages
for angels and devils
with the sun's rays
spotlighting their performance

her browned skin
roped around it all
purple eyes under
blue shadows

and the clouds roll in and
hide the sun as if it was
up to her now
to
shine, and
the ground she walks on
kisses her feet with every step.

I know this
because I hear
the smack and pucker

grow more
pronounced as she comes
closer.

and I wouldn't
be writing this
if she hadn't glanced my way

but there are some good things
that just break your heart.

the women of my life

oh, they let me live with this

this clockwork clawing at the
cavities of my heart
this cobwebbed trance filled
with jesters and
bad comedians directing entire sets
at my hidden scars
this hollow throat where boats of acid
careen down
into the pit of my belly
this tyrannical obsessive brain
all the way to the crust
left on a peanut butter and jelly
sandwich

this purge
this pain

this blank stare at walls
and construction workers
and couples in love and
people on trains
and pigeons on sills and roadkill on steps
and nothing in particular.
this emptiness that consumes
the rest of the emptiness.

they ignore my calls.
my attempts to apologize
and let bygones be

while they dance
in living rooms draped across

the arms
of new men
with nicer clothes, softer smiles,
better methods of
showing them what affection I
never could.

they have forgotten the good times,
but even worse
they have forgotten the bad.

and they just move on,
leaving me with
nothing else to do but
live with this.

my balance

in a storm you are
a lighthouse.

in a drought
you are a storm.

socks

morning coffee
rests in hand.
it is warm to
my palm.
back yard I stand.
the birds moan and
I get it.
the clothes line
holds socks.
hers not mine.
I wonder
how pathetic it would be
if I asked her
to pick them up
but that would require
her to
come back.

for august (i think was her name)

unassumingly liberated
smoking shorts
on the fire escape
her auburn hair
catching
the ghost
of the tobacco.

curious mind

a barge barrels
over the Hudson.

it moves smoothly
steadfastly
along and
pushes the water
and the fish
out of its way.

it doesn't look backward
or
toward Jersey or
Manhattan.
it has its mission.

what strikes me most
is the steam
flowing carefree
from it.

it doesn't go
as the barge goes.
it climbs up the
George Washington Bridge
to greet the cars
and faces.

it huddles among the
flowers at Riverbank.
it tangles and tangos
with the wind.

peculiar
to think that
the engine which fuels and
propels the machine
has its own
curious mind.

it is like you in that way.

exterminator

everyone back in the boondocks
sucked on buffet crab cakes
and envied
where I laid my head
and told me to take a lover.

I was tucked away behind the street
in that old place, alone
a filthy pretty slush bucket
of an apartment.

and they'd say "wow! New York City!"
and next door, the homeless man
would piss into the sun
catching the synagogue in the line of fire.

Leonard Cohen lived across the street
once.
his ghost peered at me
through the blinds on Sundays
(R.I.P. you son of a bitch - stop pitying me)

and I would tell the people back home
about Leonard's ghost
and the ones that knew nothing
of this city or who I really am
knew nothing of him either

and they all envied me
for the wrong reasons.

they would say "ahhhhhh New York City!"
like it was some magical
fairy fuck fest
with hot movie stars and lights and money
and romance
"get you some of that romance! ohhh, the romance!"

but in reality
I was sleeping with the bed bugs.

and thankfully
they loved me
better than the women did that rolled in and out
like a DMV in Detroit.

there's Kristen, Jasmine, Lena, Britney
Tony, Jane, Georgia
crawling up my pillow

burrowing into my hip
biting off pieces of me, the skin of the literal.

and then they would disappear
into the morning, back into the mattress.
clichés, all of them.
but that's basically it for this city, played out
in the form of a bug.
and what's the difference anyway, because

tomorrow, the exterminator
is set
to appear, and he will blast
the corners of my
8ft x 8ft
city
and destroy all love left over.

he is god
or he plays it well.

toxic ending

my lazy love letters were consumed
by the cats, instead of her eyes.

she refused to indulge my narcissism.
she was always so smart.

"your soul is full of sludge" she said.
"you are toxic."
this, I knew.

dandelions in the backyard withered
as I chased her down to the pond.
the frogs keeled over
in between the ribbiting
and the birds fell from the sky like
hail and promises.

everything surrounding me eventually
perished

and that Sunday afternoon
I swore that I would not
let her.

reservoir

we walked the park reservoir.
I glanced at the hand
I had not
held in weeks.

"do something. be something.
for her. do it for her."
I thought
but I didn't.

ducks swam
toward our feet.
I had no bread.
I had forgotten.

night came, and
closing our eyes
meant
we could finally
separate.

I wish it were
our nightmare
but I think it was
our peace.

i am hopeless

I write this
on the train to all
the women who have
broken me.

there is one of them now
right there
leaning against the pole
reading Mark Twain
yawning
in
slow
motion.

aftermath

three years in the darkness
and we didn't flinch
even once.

no, not once
unlike
the moths spooked at the bulb
or the frogs rolling over under quiet willows.

no, we didn't withdraw from it.

instead, we ate table scraps
and survived the attrition.
we laughed into the
pilgrimage and
kicked rocks at the desolation.
the cockroach whose company we kept
was named Kevin
and he borrowed our milk.
the flower in the window became all thorn
after it had no choice but to wilt.

since you've gone, though
I've forgotten such courage.

oh, what this man was
that I didn't know this man could be.

if you're out there reading this
are you still such
a woman?

love is a dirty, shitty thing
to reveal our
potential

and then to take it all away
when it goes.

to love you

to love you is to
live out full lives every day.
it is to consume the morning sunlight
like rivers of ice cream. it is to
flirt with madness behind
the velvet cloak of a drowning night.
it is to ride with the bull
into the coldest corner of this canyon.
it is to punch our way toward the
end of this timeline. it is to find
Death loitering in the foyer
waiting to greet us
ashamed of himself.
and it is to go kicking and screaming
but smiling and still loving
regardless.

a note:

to be enough for someone
in a world of greed
is everything.

god

I have been looking
for God
for years.
I search again today.

"I don't expect I'll ever
find God" I lament
to myself
as I run over a girl
swerving listless
along the sidewalk

her eyes buried
in the Sunday Times

hair like autumn fire
distinguished and
inextinguishable

and a smile that punches me
in the square of my gut.

I should ask her to coffee
and see if she has
discovered God yet.

necessary journey

you will bleed
to find
the love that you deserve.

you will suffer slow and
you will scream at the
unforgiving gods
as they laugh.

you will break up
you will break down, then
you will wake up
and repeat.

it
is just part of
it.

there is no shortcut.

but once that love is yours
it will heal every wound
that this necessary journey
left.

where are the words for closure?

if i could only write
one more poem
worth a damn

I could move on.

one last spill of the guts.

one last embarrassing letter
tossed at the feet
of the masses.

I won't be happy
until
I feel
naked and shriveled
in front of
them all

and the birds have circled up
to pick through
my lungs

and the clocks have
chased off
the beautiful

(but
        forgettable)
blonde Sirens of summer.

I won't be happy
I won't be happy.

one more piece that
makes sense for us

not just for the sales.
can you imagine?

and don't get me wrong
I don't think
this is that piece

but just know that
I'm trying.

Printed in Great Britain
by Amazon